CAROL STREAM PUBLIC LIBRARY

3 1319 00350 1449

WITHDRAWN

Carol Stream Public Library
616 Hiawatha Drive
Carol Stream, Illinois   60188

The Battle of Gettysburg

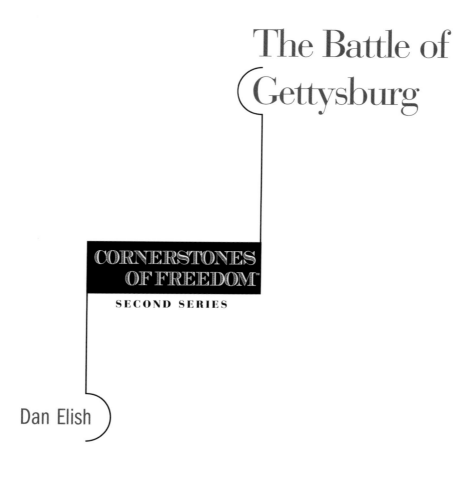

CORNERSTONES OF FREEDOM

SECOND SERIES

Dan Elish

Children's Press®
A Division of Scholastic Inc.
New York • Toronto • London • Auckland • Sydney
Mexico City • New Delhi • Hong Kong
Danbury, Connecticut

Carol Stream Public Library
Carol Stream, Illinois 60188

Photographs © 2005: Brown Brothers: 6, 11 left, 12, 16, 26, 27, 30, 35, 44 left; Corbis Images: cover top, 10, 40 (Bettmann), cover bottom (Lester Lefkowitz), 20 right (Medford Historical Society Collection), 11 right (The Corcoran Gallery of Art), 5, 9, 14, 15, 23, 33 left, 34, 36; Getty Images: 29 (MPI), 18, 33 right; Library of Congress: 4, 8, 20 left, 21, 22, 24, 28, 32, 37, 38, 39, 44 right, 45 right, 45 left; North Wind Picture Archives: 7, 25; Stock Montage, Inc.: 3, 45 center; Superstock, Inc./Stock Montage: 17; The Image Works/Topham: 31; US Army/via SODA: 13, 44 center.

Library of Congress Cataloging-in-Publication Data

Elish, Dan.

The Battle of Gettysburg / Dan Elish.

p. cm. — (Cornerstones of freedom. Second series)

Includes bibliographical references and index.

ISBN 0-516-23623-7

1. 1. Gettysburg, Battle of, Gettysburg, Pa., 1863—Juvenile literature. [1. Gettysburg, Battle of, Gettysburg, Pa., 1863.] I. Title. II. Series.

E475.53.E45 2005

973.7'349—dc22

2004010661

Copyright © 2005 Scholastic Inc.

All rights reserved. Published simultaneously in Canada.

Printed in the United States of America.

CHILDREN'S PRESS, and CORNERSTONES OF FREEDOM™, and associated logos are trademarks and or registered trademarks of Scholastic Library Publishing. SCHOLASTIC and associated logos are trademarks and or registered trademarks of Scholastic Inc.

1 2 3 4 5 6 7 8 9 10 R 14 13 12 11 10 09 08 07 06 05

J
973.7349
ELI

By July 1863, the Civil War between America's Northern and Southern states had been raging for two years. At the start of the war, the Union, or Northern forces, had been favored to win. But the Confederates (Southern forces) had succeeded in battle after battle.

2/05

At the time of the Battle of Gettysburg, General Robert E. Lee was commander of the Army of Northern Virginia. He would later become commanding general of all Confederate forces.

★ ★ ★ ★

Now the two armies were engaged at Gettysburg, Pennsylvania, located 85 miles (137 kilometers) from Washington, D.C. Two days of fighting had already left thousands dead and wounded. As dawn broke on day three, Confederate general Robert E. Lee had a daring plan. Union troops were stationed atop a ridge of four hills. From this position, they had a clear shot at the advancing Confederate forces. Even so, Lee had faith that his men could attack head on and win another victory.

A little before three in the afternoon, Confederate general George Pickett gave the order to his troops. "Up men and to your posts. Don't forget today that you are from old Virginia!" With those words 15,000 Confederate troops marched as one toward Union lines. The final fight in the Battle of Gettysburg had begun.

MARCH TOWARD WAR
In 1776, Thomas Jefferson wrote in the Declaration of Independence that American citizens were entitled to "life, liberty, and the pursuit of happiness." Unfortunately, these ideas only applied to white people. Our country's founding fathers did much to advance the cause of freedom, yet they owned about 1,400 slaves among them.

* * * *

Starting around 1789, Southern cotton **plantations** depended on slave labor. Over time, many Northerners came to view slavery as wrong. This difference in opinion would eventually lead to a deep divide within the country.

The North and South shared different ideas about governing as well. The South believed in states' rights. They felt that the laws of each individual state were more important than the laws of the federal, or national, government. On the other hand, most Northerners believed that the government in Washington, D.C. had the right to tell each state what it could and could not do. Through the years, a series of **compromises** were created in hopes of satisfying both sides.

Members of the U.S. House of Representatives debate the subject of slavery.

5

Lincoln was against the spread of slavery. His views on slavery made him unpopular among many Southerners.

THE RISE OF ABRAHAM LINCOLN

In 1858, a lawyer from Illinois named Abraham Lincoln ran for the United States Senate. Lincoln was a Republican. This new political party was mostly made up of people who were against the spread of slavery.

Lincoln's opponent was Democrat Stephen Douglas. Douglas believed that new territories should have the right to decide for themselves whether to allow slavery or not. But Lincoln felt differently. He said, "A house divided against itself cannot stand. . . . I believe this government cannot **endure** permanently half slave and half free." Douglas won the election, but the American people were impressed with Lincoln's intelligence, wit, and **integrity**. Two years later, he was elected president of the United States.

Many white people in the South were not pleased by Lincoln's election. After years of tension and disagreement, this was the last straw. On December 20, 1860, South Carolina seceded,

UNCLE TOM'S CABIN

In 1852, a writer named Harriet Beecher Stowe published a novel called *Uncle Tom's Cabin*. It describes the terrible conditions in which slaves lived. Stowe's book was a huge success and is credited with raising awareness of slavery's horrors. Stowe met President Abraham Lincoln during the Civil War. He supposedly said to her, "So you're the little woman who wrote the book that started this great war."

6

The Lincoln-Douglas debate was held at Knox College in Galesburg, Illinois. The debates attracted the attention of the entire nation.

After Lincoln's election, a group of Southerners raised a flag of independence in Savannah, Georgia, in November 1860.

or withdrew, from the Union. Within two months, six other Southern states followed. Four more states later joined them. Together, they formed a new nation called the Confederate States of America.

Upon taking office, Lincoln did not want to be the one to start a war. But it wasn't long before Lincoln received word that Fort Sumter in South Carolina's Charleston Harbor was running low on food. After Lincoln sent Union ships to resupply the fort, Southern **artillery** fired on the fort. The bloodiest war in American history had begun.

THE BATTLE OF BULL RUN

When the war began, most people believed that the Union would win easily. After all, the North had twenty-three states compared to the Confederacy's eleven. The North also had about 22 million people, one hundred thousand factories, and 20,000 miles (32,187 km) of railroad track. The Confederacy had a population of 9 million, which included 4 million slaves. The South had only 20,000 factories and 9,000 miles (14,484 km) of railroad track.

Confederate forces fired on Fort Sumter on April 12, 1861. It marked the beginning of the Civil War.

Even so, the Confederacy had some advantages. Union troops had to invade and conquer the South to claim victory. The Confederacy only had to defend its eleven states. In addition, most Southern soldiers were raised on farms and knew how to use a gun. Also, America's best military commanders were from the South.

The First Battle of Bull Run at Manassas Junction, Virginia, was a rude awakening for the Union. At first, the Union fought the Rebels to a standoff. Then a regiment of Confederate **reinforcements** arrived. For the first time, the Northern troops heard the terrifying "rebel yell," the

Three Confederate soldiers of the Third Georgia Infantry posed for this portrait in July 1862.

Confederate soldiers charge Union troops during the First Battle of Bull Run.

BIRTH OF A NICKNAME

It is said that during the First Battle of Bull Run, Confederate general Barnard Bee cried to his troops, "There stands Jackson like a stone wall! Rally behind the Virginians!" From then on, General Thomas Jackson, one of the best and fiercest generals in the Civil War, became known as "Stonewall" Jackson. A few months before the Battle of Gettysburg, he was accidentally killed by one of his own men. Some historians believe that the outcome of Gettysburg and possibly the entire war may have been different if Jackson had lived.

Thomas "Stonewall" Jackson had the unique ability to inspire his troops to victory.

scream of the Confederate troops as they charged. Soon the Union troops were running for their lives. They were followed by reporters and picnickers who had come to watch. As one newsman wrote, "All sense of manhood seemed to be forgotten. . . . Every **impediment** to flight was cast aside. Rifles, bayonets, pistols . . . cartridge-boxes, canteens, blankets, and over-coats lined the road."

Although General George B. McClellan had attended the West Point Military Academy, he did not prove to be an effective army commander.

★ ★ ★ ★
LINCOLN'S GENERALS

The first two years of the Civil War were marked by President Lincoln's desperate search for a good general. After the loss at Bull Run, Lincoln handed the Union troops over to a young general named George B. McClellan. As it turned out, McClellan was extremely shy about taking the fight to the South. He spent eight months whipping the Union troops into shape before launching a single attack. When the Union army finally moved, it suffered a series of losses. One unknown Union soldier said after a defeat, "The slaughter is terrible; the result is disastrous. Until we have good generals it is useless to fight battles."

Still, the Union troops held their own in some battles. In September 1862, General Lee tried to invade Maryland. This action led to the Battle of Antietam. With more than 23,000 dead and wounded, it was the single bloodiest day in the war. When Lee retreated, Lincoln declared victory.

A Union soldier assists his wounded comrade.

Lincoln then issued the Emancipation Proclamation, an order that freed all slaves in the Confederacy. This order paved the way for 180,000 African American troops to eventually join the Union army. But these new soldiers didn't help the North in the coming battles. Commanded by General Ambrose E. Burnside, Union forces suffered a

THE UNION AND CONFEDERATE ARMIES

The Army of the Potomac was the main Union army. The Army of Northern Virginia was the main Confederate force. Each army was organized roughly the same way:

- A *corps* (pronounced "core") was the largest single group in the army, consisting of more than 60,000 men.

- Each corps was split into three *divisions*.

- Each division was split into two to four *brigades*.

- Each brigade was composed of four to six *regiments*.

- Each regiment was divided into ten *companies*.

- Each company was divided into two *platoons*.

14

African American guards of the 107th United States Colored Troops pose outside a guardhouse in Virginia. By the end of the Civil War, about 179,000 black men served as soldiers in the U.S. Army.

defeat at Fredericksburg in December 1862. Then they launched an offensive against Southern troops at Chancellorsville. Lee brilliantly divided his army and attacked the Union on both sides. When it was all over, the North had lost another 17,000 men.

Confederate spirits were riding high. Lee figured that he could win the war with one more major battle. He hoped the next fight would break the Union's will and bring peace to the Confederacy.

LEADING TO GETTYSBURG

In the late spring of 1863, General Lee's Army of Northern Virginia was at full strength. It had 85,000 men in uniform. The Northern Union Army of the Potomac was down to 95,000 men. (Union soldiers were also known as "bluecoats" due to the color of their uniforms.) But Lee knew that the North would eventually gather a much greater force and fight its way to the Confederate capital at Richmond, Virginia. The time to win was now.

Lee decided to attack southern Pennsylvania. He thought that a Confederate victory would give strength to a group of northerners called copperheads. These were men and women who wanted Lincoln to settle for a **negotiated** peace. This meant that fighting would stop and the South would be allowed to exist as its own country.

This illustration shows a Confederate army camp at White Springs, Virginia.

Lincoln spent the first part of the war searching for the right general. He is shown here visiting General McClellan and his troops after the Battle of Antietam in 1862.

Lee also thought that a win in Northern territory would demonstrate the strength of the Confederacy. He hoped it would encourage England and France to send his troops greatly needed supplies. If the Southern troops did especially well, they might even be able to capture the cities of Harrisburg or Baltimore and demand a peace treaty.

Despite Lee's impressive record of victories, President Lincoln was also confident. But he was still looking for the right general. "We cannot help beating them," he told Secretary of the Navy Gideon Welles, "if we have the man."

Lincoln's general at the time was Joseph Hooker. On June 28, just three days before the Battle

Meade's large eyes and quick temper earned him the nickname "the snapping turtle."

of Gettysburg began, Hooker resigned. Lincoln then promoted Major General George Gordon Meade. Lincoln thought that Meade would be more forceful than other Union generals in taking the battle directly to the enemy. Even Lee saw the wisdom of the move. He told his staff, "General Meade will make no **blunder** in my front, and if I make one, he will make haste to take advantage of it."

Confederate General Jeb Stuart leads his cavalry on a scouting expedition. Today, Stuart is considered one of the greatest cavalry commanders in American history.

GENERAL JEB STUART

Now Lee turned to one of his most trusted generals, Jeb Stuart. Stuart had beaten Union troops in battle after battle. One of the most colorful soldiers in the Civil War, Stuart was famous for wearing fancy hats, knee-high boots, and a red-lined cape into battle.

Stuart led Lee's cavalry, or soldiers on horseback. During the Civil War, cavalry was used mostly to sneak behind enemy lines and scout out positions. In the last few days of June, Lee asked Stuart to take his cavalry into Pennsylvania and look for Union troops. Stuart was to remain in contact with Lee.

Stuart left on June 26. He soon discovered that the roads he wanted to use were already taken by Union forces. Instead of quietly scouting the Union position, Stuart attacked. He captured a supply train and wreaked havoc on the Union army. In the process Stuart got separated from the rest of the Army of Virginia for a full week. As a result, Lee was not able to get the information he needed from Stuart. Lee had no idea where the Union army was headed.

THE APPROACHING BATTLE

After the death of his best general, Stonewall Jackson, Lee reorganized his Army of Virginia. He created three corps of three divisions each. The first division was commanded by his highest-ranking general, James Longstreet. The second was under the command of A. P. Hill. The third was led by Richard "Baldy" Ewell.

Even without Stuart's information, Confederate forces continued to march north. They found little resistance. On June 26, Ewell's corps crossed the Potomac River into Maryland and then continued on to Pennsylvania. On June 28, Lee led the rest of the army into Chambersburg, only 25 miles (40 km) from Gettysburg. Lee knew he needed to attack Union troops soon, before Meade had the chance to take full control of his army. The trouble was that Lee still didn't know where the Union army was hiding. He needed information from Stuart now more than ever.

General Henry Heth was ordered to march toward Gettysburg to find out where Union forces were stationed.

SEARCHING FOR SHOES

One of the most famous legends surrounding the Battle of Gettysburg concerns General Henry Heth's advance division. By this point in the war, the Confederate army was in desperate need of basic supplies. As the story goes, Heth and his men came to Gettysburg in search of shoes. But many historians believe that General Heth made up the shoe story to explain why he accidentally ran into Union forces.

★ ★ ★ ★

As it turned out, General Meade and his troops were in Maryland. Meade knew that the Confederate troops were headed toward Gettysburg. On June 30 Meade sent two brigades of cavalry, led by General John Buford, to occupy the town. At the same time, Meade ordered his entire army to Gettysburg.

Meanwhile, Jeb Stuart still hadn't returned. After getting information from a spy, Lee sent out a division under the command of General Henry Heth. The division would march ahead down a road called Chambersburg Pike toward Gettysburg. Heth's orders were simply to see where the Union forces were stationed. He was not to engage in battle until the entire Confederate army had time to gather.

This photograph shows the town of Gettysburg and its surrounding fields as it looked in 1863.

GETTYSBURG, DAY ONE

On July 1, at 6 A.M., Heth's men came down Chambersburg Pike and ran right into Buford's Union cavalry. The Confederates attacked, and the first shots of Gettysburg were fired.

The Confederates outnumbered Buford's forces by two to one. Just when it looked as though the Union forces would be completely overrun, General John F. Reynolds came galloping across the field followed by two brigades. Reynolds realized the importance of high terrain, or ground. He expertly positioned the Union reinforcements along Seminary Ridge. He also sent word back to General Meade that the main army should hurry. No sooner had Reynolds given his orders than he was shot dead.

Reynolds was replaced by General Abner Doubleday. For a time, Union troops held their ground. But as the fighting raged on, the tide turned back to the South. Overwhelmed, Union armies reeled back through the town itself. By this time, the Union forces were under the command of General Winfield Hancock. Hancock ordered that the Union forces regroup atop Cemetery Hill, a hill just outside of town.

This statue honors John Burns, a resident of Gettysburg who joined the first day's battle.

A LOCAL HERO

John Burns was a seventy-two-year-old shoemaker in Gettysburg. When the battle began, Burns picked up a musket from a wounded soldier and fought for the Union army all day. He was wounded three times. He later became the oldest person honored by a Civil War monument.

Union troops came to Cemetery Hill, shown here, to regroup after the first day's battle.

By this point, General Lee had arrived. He ordered Ewell to keep after the retreating Union forces "if he found it practicable." Ewell took stock of the situation. His troops were hot and tired. He could see that the Union position was good, and he suspected that Union reinforcements were nearby. Ewell decided to withdraw. Today, some historians believe that the Confederates could have driven the Northern troops out of Gettysburg that first day. Due to Ewell's caution, Union troops had a full night to regroup and dig in to their positions.

DAY TWO, PREPARING TO ATTACK

As dawn broke on July 2, General Meade stood on Cemetery Hill and talked with his corps commanders. Union troops were already in position on Cemetery Hill and nearby Culp's Hill. But Meade knew they could strengthen their position even more. They decided to place Union troops along the two-mile (3.2-km) length of Cemetery Ridge to two hills south of town, now called Round Top and Little Round Top. In order to attack, the Confederate army would be forced to cross low ground with almost no cover.

On the Confederate side, General Lee was eager to fight. He gave his orders: Longstreet would attack the Union left near the Round Tops. Ewell's forces would attack the Union right.

This illustration shows the view from the summit of Little Round Top, where Union troops were positioned. Advancing Confederate troops would have nowhere to hide.

As Longstreet and Ewell got their troops into position General Meade made sure that his four hills were well manned. He assigned the defense of the two Round Tops to Dan Sickles. But Sickles felt that the Round Tops were too

General James Longstreet gives orders to his troops on the second day of battle.

From the summit of Little Round Top, Union General G. K. Warren spotted Confederates approaching and called for reinforcements.

far from the action. He disobeyed orders and moved his troops to a grove of peach orchards he felt were on higher ground. By doing this, Sickles left the Round Tops exposed to a Confederate attack.

Luckily for the North, it took Longstreet a long time to get his troops in position. At 3 P.M., General Meade finally got word that Dan Sickles had disobeyed orders. But with Confederate troops readying for attack, it was too late. There was no time left for Sickles to get his troops back into position.

HEROIC ACTS

At the first sound of guns, General Meade sent one of his chief aides, General Gouverneur K. Warren, to Little Round Top. When Warren saw Confederate rifle barrels glinting in the late afternoon sun, he sent for immediate reinforcements. It was a critical decision that probably saved the day for the Union.

Fierce fighting took place on Little Round Top as the Union tried to defend its position.

As two Confederate regiments marched on Little Round Top, four Union regiments raced as fast as they could up the side of the hill. The tail end of the Union line was anchored

* * * *

by the 20th Maine. This regiment was under the command of Colonel Joshua L. Chamberlain. Chamberlain was a thirty-three-year-old language professor at Bowdoin College. His orders were "to hold that ground at all hazards." The fighting was fierce. Chamberlain later said, "My dead and wounded were nearly as great in number as those still on duty. . . . The ground was soaked with blood."

With a third of his men down and practically out of ammunition, Chamberlain made a daring decision. He cried, "Fix bayonets!" and the men of the 20th Maine charged. The Confederates were so surprised that some of them surrendered. At the same time, another Union regiment opened fire, and Little Round Top held.

Fighting was just as fierce up and down Cemetery Ridge. Some of the hardest fighting took place on a patch of land called Devil's Den, which was covered with boulders. Inch by inch, Confederate troops pushed the Union forces back. Desperate, Union general Hancock turned to the 1st Minnesota Volunteers,

Union soldiers lay dead on the field of battle.

a small regiment of 262 men. He cried, "Advance, Colonel, and take those colors!" Later, William Lochren, a Minnesota man, remembered:

> *Every man realized in an instant what the order meant—death or wounds to us all; the sacrifice of the regiment to gain a few minutes time and save the position, and probably the battlefield—and every man saw and accepted the necessity for the sacrifice.*

The Minnesotans fixed bayonets and charged. Out of 262 men, 215 went down, either dead or wounded. No one deserted. The line held until Union reinforcements arrived.

The fighting continued into the night. Union and Rebel troops snuck in and around the boulders of Devil's Den, attacking each other with bayonets. By the end of the day's fighting, 15,000 men were dead or wounded. As Confederate and Union men searched through the darkness for wounded soldiers, Meade and Lee took stock of their positions. The Confederate army had almost broken through enemy lines several times, but the Union position along Cemetery Ridge had held.

DAY THREE

As dawn broke on July 3, Lee was eager to continue the fight. For two days in a row, the Army of Northern Virginia had come close to beating the Union troops. Lee hadn't given up hope. He still believed that one big victory could turn the tide of the war.

Lee's first plan of attack centered on taking Culp's Hill. Ewell had spent the night preparing Confederate forces for a morning **assault**. But at 4:30 A.M., the Union army struck first. They were determined to recapture a line of trenches they had lost in the previous day's battle.

Culp's Hill was the scene of fierce fighting on the morning of July 3.

General Armstrong Custer was a fearless leader. He would later lose his life in a famous battle with the Sioux Indians at Little Big Horn in 1876.

* * * *

Again, fighting was fierce. One regiment lost nearly 250 men in just a few minutes. After hours of brutal conflict, the Union line held. At 11 A.M., the Confederates finally pulled back.

Lee's second plan of attack called on the talents of Jeb Stuart. Stuart had finally returned with his cavalry to the main Confederate army the day before. Early in the morning of day three, Stuart led six thousand men south. His plan was to circle around the Union flank, then attack from behind.

Early in the afternoon, however, Stuart ran into five thousand Northern troops. One Union brigade was under the command of General George Armstrong Custer. Custer had graduated last in his class at West Point Military Academy. However, he was a brilliant cavalry officer. Again and again, Stuart and Custer charged. One soldier from Pennsylvania remembered the scene:

As the two columns approached each other, the pace of each increased. . . . So sudden and violent was the collision that many of the horses were turned end over end and crushed their riders beneath them. The clashing of sabers, the firing of pistols, and demands for surrender, and cries of combatants filled the air.

This illustration shows Lee surrounded by his generals. Lee hoped to bring the battle to an end with one final, daring attack on the Union army.

At one point, Custer's horse was shot out from under him. He mounted another horse and continued to fight. Again, the Union line held.

PICKETT'S CHARGE

Though Confederate attempts to break through the Union lines had failed, the Confederate army wasn't finished. Early that morning Lee had ridden with Longstreet to the top of Cemetery Ridge. They could see the Union lines from there. Lee wanted Longstreet's men to attack the Union army head-on. To support the attack, Lee would use massive bursts of cannon fire.

GEORGE PICKETT

George Pickett only commanded three out of the nine divisions that made the final, fateful march on the Union lines. Still, he received the blame for the attack's failure. In later years, Pickett bitterly blamed General Lee, saying, "The old man had my division slaughtered."

George Pickett's name has always been associated with the failed assault on Union forces, which is often called "Pickett's Charge."

★ ★ ★ ★

Longstreet thought it was a terrible idea. He said to Lee, "It is my opinion that no fifteen thousand men ever **arrayed** for battle can take that position." Lee reminded Longstreet that the Rebel army had overcome similar odds before. Again, Longstreet objected. But Lee was convinced that the Union army would crack. He ordered Longstreet to assemble his troops. Three divisions were put under the charge of George Pickett, a general who had never led a division into actual combat.

At one in the afternoon, Confederate cannons opened fire. The sound was so loud that some people claimed to have heard the explosions all the way in Pittsburgh, 185 miles (298 km) away. The attack seemed impressive, but most of the shells landed behind the Union army's front lines. They missed the main body of troops and hit staff officers, supply tents, hospitals, and horses instead.

Soon after, the Union artillery came back with its own cannon fire. But Union general Henry Hunt soon held back some cannons in order to save ammunition. He also hoped to trick the Confederates into thinking that their cannon fire had hit its marks.

* * * *

Cannons such as these were useful for attacking wide open spaces of enemy territory.

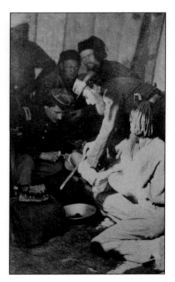

BATTLEFIELD SURGERY

By the time of the Civil War, no medicine had yet been invented to fight infection. A good battlefield **surgeon** had to work fast. The best surgeons could remove a wounded limb in a few minutes.

Army doctors perform surgery in a makeshift hospital during the war.

The trick worked. At 3 P.M., Confederate colonel E. P. Alexander reported to General George Pickett that there was a hole in the Union lines. Pickett turned to Longstreet and asked, "Shall I advance?" Longstreet nodded, but he was certain that the plan was doomed to fail. Pickett turned to his men and gave the order.

Three divisions marched at a steady pace into the open field. From Cemetery Ridge, the Union army could see all

Confederate forces charged Cemetery Hill, starting the final assault of the Battle of Gettysburg.

15,000 men marching toward them. One Union colonel called it, "The most beautiful thing I ever saw."

But then the battle began. Union troops opened fire from Little Round Top and Cemetery Hill. Rebel soldiers went down in bunches. When the Confederate troops were within 200 yards (183 meters), hundreds of Union muskets went off at once. Entire Rebel lines fell. Still the Confederates kept coming. They struggled toward a stone wall where the Union line was thought to be weakest.

The fighting was wild and confusing. Union regiments ran over to help. One soldier remembered, "We just rushed in like wild beasts. Men swore and cursed and struggled and fought, grappled in hand-to-hand fight, threw stones, clubbed their muskets, kicked, yelled, and hurrahed." The Union forces proved to be too strong for the Confederates.

Later, Lee rode out to meet his retreating troops. He took complete blame for the failure, saying, "It was all my fault."

Chaotic battle led to the capture of a Confederate brigade.

★ ★ ★ ★

Still, he begged his men to get back in ranks and prepare for a possible Union **counterattack**. But when Lee asked Pickett to place his division back in line, Pickett replied, "General Lee, I have no division."

At the end of the three-day battle, more than 51,000 thousand men (23,000 Union and 28,000 Confederate) were

A group of dead Confederate soldiers await burial at Gettysburg.

killed, wounded, or missing at Gettysburg. As the surviving troops regrouped and left town, Gettysburg homes were turned into hospitals and funeral homes. Horses were piled up and burned. Men were hastily buried. In years to come, farmers were forced to plant around the bodies of dead soldiers or else face digging them up for reburial.

THE GETTYSBURG ADDRESS

The Union had won a major victory, but President Lincoln wasn't satisfied. When Meade reported to the president that the enemy was in retreat, Lincoln cried, "My God, is that all?" He believed that the Union should have counterattacked and completed the victory. But Meade thought his troops were too tired. He refused. As a result, Lee was able to march back to Virginia and rally his troops. They went on to fight for another two years.

On November 19, the Soldiers' National Cemetery at Gettysburg was **dedicated**. The main speaker was Edward Everett. Everett was a former secretary of state and United States senator. President Lincoln was also asked to say a

Everett was considered one of the best orators, or public speakers, of his day. At the dedication of Gettysburg National Cemetery, his speech lasted more than two hours.

Gettysburg National Cemetery was created to properly bury the Union soldiers who died in the battle.

ENVELOPES

Popular myth says that Lincoln wrote his famous Gettysburg Address on the back of an envelope while traveling by train to the battlefield. That is almost certainly not true. Lincoln was known to write his speeches carefully and well ahead of time.

"few appropriate remarks." Lincoln accepted the invitation, partly because he was looking for a chance to express his thoughts on the Union's purpose in the war.

Edward Everett spoke first. His speech lasted two hours. Then Lincoln stood up and delivered his famous Gettysburg Address in just three minutes.

Today, Lincoln's short speech is thought to be one of the best in American history. In a time of great divisions between North and South and black and white, Lincoln stated that the mission of the United States was to be a country where "all men are created equal." He also referred to America as "a nation." This made it clear that America was a unified country, not a collection of states.

A TURNING POINT

Many historians feel that the Battle of Gettysburg was the turning point of the Civil War. When General Lee's attempt to invade the North failed, so did his hopes of receiving aid from England and France. He also knew there was no chance of negotiating for peace.

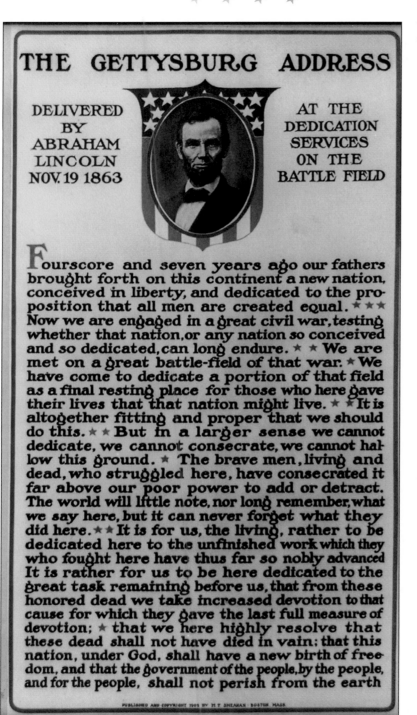

This is the text of Abraham Lincoln's famous Gettysburg Address.

General Ulysses S. Grant was appointed General-in-Chief of the Union army in March 1864. One year later, Lee would surrender to Grant at Appomattox Courthouse in Virginia.

Going into the battle, Lee knew that the South needed a big win. He knew that the North would soon become a better fighting force. It would also learn make full use of its advantages in industry and manpower.

He was right. After Gettysburg, Lee was forced to retreat to the South. President Lincoln then promoted a general named Ulysses S. Grant to command the Army of the Potomac, and the tide turned toward the North. On April 9, 1865, General Robert E. Lee surrendered to Ulysses Grant at the Appomattox Court House in Virginia.

The years directly following the war are known as Reconstruction, or a time of rebuilding. Much of the war had been fought in the South, and parts of the region were in ruins. The war also brought about changes in government. The Northern Congress passed a series of laws and amendments to the Constitution. These laws were supposed to protect the rights of blacks. Unfortunately, blacks continued to be denied their basic rights for a long time. Slavery was illegal, but blacks were not allowed to vote. They were banned from "white-only" restaurants, schools, public restrooms, and other places. It took until the 1960s before black Americans were guaranteed basic civil rights.

Today, the United States has made great progress in making sure that all of its citizens are treated fairly. Still, it remains one of America's greatest challenges to live up to Abraham Lincoln's promise of being a country "dedicated to the **proposition** that all men are created equal."

Glossary

arrayed—set out for display or use

artillery—a section of an army that is armed with guns

assault—an attack upon a person or an army

blunder—a careless mistake

compromise—when two or more parties each give up something they want in order to reach agreement

counterattack—an attack against an enemy in order to regain what was lost

dedicated—set aside for a particular purpose

endure—to last

impediment—something that gets in the way or prevents something from happening

integrity—great honesty and moral strength

negotiated—brought about a settlement through discussion and compromise

plantation—a farm where crops are grown in large numbers

proposition—something that is offered for consideration and acceptance

reinforcements—fresh troops that strengthen or relieve an army that is engaged in combat

surgeon—a doctor who is skilled in performing surgery, or operations

Timeline: The Battle of

1860

NOVEMBER
Abraham Lincoln is elected the sixteenth president of the United States.

DECEMBER
South Carolina secedes from the Union.

1861

APRIL
Confederate guns fire on Union ships at Fort Sumter. The Civil War begins.

1862

SEPTEMBER
Lincoln issues the Emancipation Proclamation, promising freedom to all slaves in the Confederacy.

DECEMBER
Confederate forces defeat Union troops at Fredericksburg.

1863

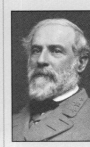

JUNE
Confederate commander Robert E. Lee decides to invade the North to force the Union into negotiating an end to the war.

JUNE
President Lincoln accepts General Joseph Hooker's resignation. He places General George Meade in command of the Army of the Potomac.

Gettysburg

1865

JULY 1
The Battle of Gettysburg begins.

JULY 2
After fierce fighting around Round Top and Little Round Top, the Peach Orchard, Culp's Hill, and Devil's Den, the North manages to hold their ground.

JULY 3
"Pickett's Charge" is stopped by Northern troops. The South retreats back to Virginia.

NOVEMBER
President Lincoln travels to a dedication ceremony at Gettysburg. He delivers his famous Gettysburg Address.

APRIL
Nearly two years after the Battle of Gettysburg, the South finally surrenders. The Civil War is over.

To Find Out More

BOOKS AND JOURNALS

McGowen, Tom. *Surrender at Appomattox*. Danbury, CT: Children's Press, 2004.

Murphy, Jim. *The Long Road to Gettysburg*. New York: Clarion Books, 1992.

Stanchak, John. *Eyewitness: Civil War*. New York: Dorling Kindersley, 2000.

ONLINE SITES

Gettysburg National Military Park's Civil War Page for Kids
http://www.nps.gov/gett/gettkidz/kidzindex.htm

PBS Historical Document: The Gettysburg Address
http://www.pbs.org/civilwar/war/gettysburg_address.html

U.S. National Archives and Records Administration, Pictures of the Civil War
http://www.archives.gov/research_room/research_topics/civil_war/civil_war_photos.html#activities

Index

Bold numbers indicate illustrations.

About the Author

Dan Elish is the author of numerous books for children, including *The Worldwide Dessert Contest* and *Born Too Short: The Confessions of an Eighth-Grade Basket Case*, which was picked as a 2003 Book for the Teen Age by the New York Public Library. He lives in New York City with his wife and daughter.